Word Fall

Also by Betty McKenzie-Tubb and published by Ginninderra Press

Meanderings

Betty McKenzie-Tubb

Word Fall

Acknowledgements

My thanks to my writing friends and to my family for their listening ears and their encouragement.

My particular thanks to Jen Gibson, who once again has given me her precious time and the use of her technological skills, and to Robyn Mathison for her meticulous reading of my verse.

Of course I am immensely grateful to Stephen Matthews and Ginninderra Press for agreeing to publish what is, since I am an octogenarian, probably my swansong.

The following poems were first published in *Poetry Matters*, edited by Cheryl Howard: 'Double Delusion', 'Alive but not counting', 'The tragic', 'Is it well with the young man?', 'Downfall', 'Postmortem', 'When I'm Old I Shall Wear Purple'.

Word Fall
ISBN 978 1 74027 503 7
Copyright © Betty McKenzie-Tubb 2018
Cover design: Betty McKenzie-Tubb

First published 2018 by
Ginninderra Press
PO Box 3461 Port Adelaide 5015 Australia
www.ginninderrapress.com.au

Contents

You cannot will a poem	7
Loss and Love	**9**
Rose Dust	11
'Is it well with the young man?'	12
Remembering 2003	13
The tragic	14
'First Vertu…'	15
For K.B.	16
The ravelled sleave	18
More than kisses	19
Dark Angel	20
Spring song for an ageing lover	21
How are you?	22
O tempora! O mores	23
Living life backwards	24
With Serious Intent	**25**
Going with the flow 1	27
Going with the flow 2	28
Homicidal gardener	29
Double delusion	30
A young girl in Sydney, 1945	31
Psalm 98	32
Suddenness	33
Magpie	35
Raga	36
An ideal marriage	37
The Miracle	38
Carpe Diem	39
Who has taken my world?	40

Alive but not counting	42
Sons of Clovis	44

Froth and Bubble — 45

Excuse	47
Excuse	49
Slick	50
Never the bride	54
To LG – a kind of ode	55
A rhyme in praise of the semicolon	56
Hot lips – a cautionary tale	57
'When I'm old I shall wear purple'	58
Sour grapes	59
The Resolution of a Problem	60
Downfall	61

You cannot will a poem

'Anyone can write a poem' – Anon

Borne across the air
the voice:
'you cannot will a poem'
it said.
For years the poet waited
for the muse.

Some writers lack
the luxury of time;
like MONA's Word Fall
particles appear;
glitter, seduce,
drop into the well
of no return.

Loss and Love

Rose Dust

Fresh from her bath, ready to don her black,
she sprinkles on her living flesh
'Ashes of Roses'

Once she lived near a graveyard.
Walking by, hand in hand
with her homburg-wearing grandfather,
she saw the arum lilies;
a long time after, symbols of death,
and even now the backdrop
for a sculptured head, tribute
to a dead son, in his corner of the garden.

There were no roses;
too pink, too sweet, too redolent of life,
though these days a favoured tribute to the lost.
Over urns of ashes, on mounds they bloom,
coloured crimson as if from transferred blood.

'Is it well with the young man?'

Samuel 2:19
for M.B.L.

That smiling child
rufus-haired
'christianed' by his sisters
on the front lawn
water dripping
from his elfin face.

Five years old
and stoic
plodding through the snow
from ground base
to the pinnacle
uncomplaining in the family's wake.

A young man
and passionate
the first snatch at his heart –
Rosealba –
such innocence in them both
before the eagle demons came.

Then these raged.
Prometheus could not
have suffered more;
only death with noose in hand
seemed kindest.
Oh Absalom, my son, my son.

Remembering 2003

There is no end to grief
it knows no boundaries,
does not obey the dictates
of anniversaries.
It is the stab in the back,
the stalker, breath close,
waiting to overtake.

No more pain today
than when uncalled grief
takes over in its own time.

The tragic

'You're very good at grief' she said –
my friend, who knows about it.
But it's grief that drives the pen
and voids the heart –
black tears on paper.

'First Vertu…'

'First vertu is to kepe the tonge' – Chaucer

Gagged by the one she loves
she sits in her corner, mute.
Visitors come and go
and with his dying breath
he romances them with his stories.

He leaves her, and with tongue released
she tells her own tales.
A poorer raconteur, raises fewer laughs,
and her freedom no recompense
        for the gap he's left behind.

For K.B.

'Just because (you're) dead now doesn't mean
(You) don't exist any more' – Billy Collins, 'All Eyes'

I read Billy Collins
and I think of you
signalling you didn't quite agree,
with an 'Oh, all right'
delivered in your quiet Yankee drawl.

>*Life has arrows*
>*which it aims at those*
>*who deserve better*
>*and such were you –*
>*stoic, mutely bearing*
>*the many stings.*

I read Billy Collins
and I think of you.
He likes his intoxicants
and so did you,
discerningly of course,
so he thinks of vodka soda with lemon
or pours himself a glass of frosty wine;
and I remember our Martinis
in the Oyster Bar at Circular Quay;
you walking soberly back to the hotel,
me, a little out of balance.

I read Billy Collins
and I think of you.
I wish I could write as he does.
I'd pen a verse for you on vellum,
use it as a bookmark
in my Collins anthology.

The ravelled sleave

'Sleep that knits up the ravell'd sleave of care,
The death of each day's life, sore labour's bath,
Balm of hurt minds, great nature's second course,
Chief nourisher in life's feast.' – William Shakespeare, *Macbeth*

Sleep that knits…
No, not for her.
The mind unravels,
her dreams intrude;
each weakness leaks
from the unguarded brain.

A journey's planned,
she's too late to board the plane.
Her guests arrive,
dinner's not cooked,
the table's not laid.

A race is run
and she is breathless, last.
Her clothes have gone;
she stands naked in the street –
all Freud's Christmases have come.

Always lacking, always wanting,
how can she sleep?
Though once her vanished darling
lay beside her; warm, corporeal.
She wished that she had never waked.

More than kisses

I loved the way your hair
was streaked with white
feathering the dark.

I loved the way you spoke to me,
voice low and honey brown.
I loved the way you looked at me,
the fire behind your eyes.

I loved the way your limbs
were so neatly put together,
the way they moved towards me.

Most of all I loved –
more than kisses –
the way your hand left the steering wheel,
silently found mine.

Dark Angel

a lover's lament

Like a black angel
she swept through the door,
billowing dark
the clothes that she wore.
Such a sweet night –
memory of bliss –
how could I know
there was something amiss?

At daybreak no sign
of the girl I adore
but three raven hairs
on the bathroom floor.

Spring song for an ageing lover

For the old ones – us –
It is the winter of our lives;
Nothing new in saying that.
Yet in the corner of the garden
The golden ash, lately lopped,
Is bravely bearing new, defiant buds
And your cherry tree, my darling,
Naked not long ago,
Has nippled branches
And soon will show its white ephemeral flowers.

It is joy, not hope,
This repeated wonder brings;
If you hear a sound
It is my heart that sings.

How are you?

So many years
and I still don't know
what to say.
How am I?

I am:

>a weeping lichen on a blackened bough,
>a telephone disconnected,
>unable to reach the one I love;
>a bottle shattered, spilling heart's blood,
>the back-seat passenger
>in someone else's car.

O tempora! O mores

Our young days were romantic times,
Spring love led to wedding chimes,
Kisses were rare and like champagne;
Alas! Those times won't come again.

The young are businesslike and free –
Sex with regularity –
No thrills accompany the act
(I hear they're very matter-of-fact)
What decision making there must be!
Query, 'Coffee? Tea? – or me?'

Living life backwards

Regret. Remorse.
These are thorns lodged so deep
they cannot be excised.
They have entered the bloodstream
and are part of me.
Slight poisons; they will not kill
but leach into past happiness;
circulate, enter the heart,
become part of the slow bleed of grief.

With Serious Intent

Going with the flow 1

In deference to modern mode
I'll chop up prose
and call it poetry
its like riding a bike really
being careful to balance
and not fall into the ditch
of rhyme or rhythm
or any of that old stuff
and of course to hell with punctuation
do-it-yourself (thats if you can)
it might take time and thought
and where's the space for that
a different thought for each line
that seems to be the thing
but make it sound profound

it is intensely sad
Miro with his blue and red
and bodies that are 'thinking meat'
get some therapeutic help
it is the year of fashion
beware of the seduction of haute cuisine
and haute couture
twin diseases of modernity
Ern Malley what have you done

Going with the flow   2

I should write a poem today –
 A modern poem
  With too much shape
   And without rhyme
    Or rhythm, for that matter
     But nothing stabs my heart
      Or gladdens my eye –
       Except, five rosellas
        On the rim of my bird bath –
         Just in time!

Homicidal gardener

I killed some snails today;
it was easy.
Too squeamish to squash them
I let them die slowly
in a briny bath (so little ruth!)
and felt no compunction.
After all, I'm *Homo sapiens*,
a member of the master class.
Class *Gastropoda* does me no harm
but threatens the order of my garden.

They died quietly, unless the scream
was too subliminal for human ears.
I shudder to think
should their pain be audible
my pleasure would increase,
for so it is with those
who want no aliens
in their ordered territory.

Double delusion

S/he believes in God,
In heaven and hell,
In resurrection
And judgement day;
In angels and archangels,
In marymotherofgod,
Transubstantiation;
Things New Agers deem
Ridiculous, irrational.

They believe in past lives,
Fortunes told by stars;
In crystals, palmistry,
Tarot cards, pendulums, auras
And fairies at the bottom of
The garden.

A young girl in Sydney, 1945

Joy abounded.
Spring.
Wild freesias
exuberant,
jollying through
the crowded
suburban pavements.

Iconic ferries rocking
through choppy waters;
sound, sea, waves –
fright, delight.

Meetings under the clock
at Central Station.
The promise of romance –
eyes looked
hands locked
hearts pounded.

Laughter,
laughter at nothing –
joy abounded.

Psalm 98

Oh sing unto our Ford a new song
for He has done marvellous things!
His right hand and His holy arm
have created all technology.

He desires us not to walk on pathways
and wear down our legs with forward drive,
but urges us to sit flabbily in our motor cars
and punish walkers with the toxic fumes.

He does remember all the print aversive
and supplies them with television sets.
And lest their withered legs should crumble under them
has delivered unto all, their remote controls.

Oh make joyful noise to our Ford, all ye on earth.
Sing to our Mazda, oh sing His praises!
Soon the pen, yea, even the biro,
will become gifts for future archaeologists.
The computer will require but constant tapping
and the buttons will respond and never byte.

Ford be praised that surgery's gone digital
and we can be disembowelled with robotic arms.
Let the joyous noise be not a screaming sound
but let computer geeks all clap their hands.

Our Ford will judge the world with righteousness
and all but the technocrats shall go to Hell.

Apologies to Aldous Huxley, *Brave New World*, and to the psalmist

Suddenness

1

The suddenness of the world!
Suddenly our globe is warm;
waters rise
rivers dry;
suddenly the ground is dust.

Suddenly technology takes over,
Emails proliferate,
calligraphy languishes,
conversations die;
our eyes morph into squares.

Suddenly music is atonal,
paintings called 'conceptual'
seem meaningless;
our senses somehow starved.

2

Babies spring into full beings,
our own bodies change.
Suddenly, one morning,
moles, warts, wens appear;
there are elephant folds in flesh
and we have our mother's hands.

Suddenly, suddenly,
those we love depart.
They fall like autumn leaves –
it's bleak winter.
It's often hard to remember
the suddenness of spring.

Magpie

Cruel, predator –
your song belies
your reputation.
Sweetest song I've ever heard,
one I'd choose for paradise.
Will you swoop?
Peck out my eyes?

You have known me
for years
passing this way,
you know I'll do
your chicks no harm.
'Blithe spirit', sing on.
Make my day.

Raga

I do not know your names –
little chirpers
little tweeters
little chatterboxes.

Dark and small
you are as the leaves
which you inhabit.
Not until you crowd in flight
do I see that you are avian.

No twitcher,
no ornithologist,
I cannot name you.

Does it matter?
your morning conversation
a bright start
to a grey day.

An ideal marriage

Mango trees, pandanus,
Seven hundred different
Kinds of eucalypt;
Frangipani, poinciana,
Bougainvillea –
The names alone
Their nectar on the tongue.

Black and white ducks –
Some that whistle –
Ibis, egrets, kingfishers;
Palaeolithic crocodiles
Motionless, three lidded,
Simulating sleep.

An ode, a sonnet,
Meet for these.

The jabiru dives,
Catches no fish –
But see the water lilies,
Their huge leaves
Following the sun,
The two black kites in flight;
Together yet apart,
Both heading in the same direction.

The Miracle (outside the retirement village)

There stands Joseph in his niche
still unblemished though facing out,
exposed to every passer-by.
Across the road the bus shed stands
with its blasphemy of graffiti.

> What residual awe or dread
> stayed the hands of those calligraphers?
> The remnant conscience of a former age
> when conscience was the voice of God?

Carpe Diem

Revenant, I know nothing.
I want to start again.
I want to see
as Ruskin insisted,
the details of every leaf, every flower,
every Gothic arch.

To look heavenwards to the stars
and downward
to every crack in the pavement,
seeing signs of ant cities,
of the seeding of weeds;
the beauty of an errant dandelion.

I want to question,
to learn to aver, not concur
for fear of damaging friendship.
I want to speak in many tongues;
understand the subtle differences
in thought each language brings.

I want to walk a different road,
discover the marvels of this facetted world.
I want to see beyond externals,
plumb the waters,
see what lies beneath.

All these wants; so little time –
the moment's now.

Who has taken my world?

The sky madonna blue
blank as a canvas.
Where are my snow-capped mountains
toeing the azure lakes?

Where are my angel wings,
feathers drifting away
in the unfelt wind?

Where are my dragons, my salamander,
my mackerel, my phantasmal birds –
the joys of my upward gaze?

Winter has passed:
sunlight has stolen my world.

Venus Adonis in the Golden Tulip

In the Golden Tulip
the most androgynous young man.
He might stand like Venus
in a fanned out shell,
a hand placed – so –
to enhance the mystery.

Cool in his Nehru shirt
of chalk white cotton,
in slacks of linen, light and loose,
he entered on a shaft of light.
Short blond hair and silver earring,
translucent skin and a neck
long, graceful, white.

Eve ate her apple, Adam's stuck:
Venus Adonis no candidate
for the love of any Eve.

Alive but not counting

She wakes and turns herself,
is sure that it is Saturday.
It's important that she know the day;
they may ask her.
If she doesn't know
where will she be?

Perhaps they'll ask her
to start from one hundred;
count back by sevens –
she's never been good at maths.

Shaking hands, paralysed by terror
may not fold the paper as is shown.
Firmer hands mark all the boxes –
are they crosses? Are they ticks?

This morning went about her duties;
ate breakfast, washed the dishes,
dressed, clothes all in right order;
phoned friends, wrote birthday cards
and thank you notes,
entertained at morning tea,
took the bus to town and watched a film.
'Count back by sevens'.
She needs a number square.

Alive

c o u n t i n g

1	2	3	4	5	6	7	8	9	10
11	12	13	14	15	16	17	18	19	20
21	22	23	24	25	26	27	28	29	30
31	32	33	34	35	36	37	38	39	40
41	42	43	44	45	46	47	48	49	50
51	52	53	54	55	56	57	58	59	60
61	62	63	64	65	66	67	68	69	70
71	72	73	74	75	76	77	78	79	80
81	82	83	84	85	86	87	88	89	90
91	92	93	94	95	96	97	98	99	100

b u t

not

Sons of Clovis

Everiste Vital Luminais (painter)

Tied to my bed
for some time now
I regard my unused feet
and I think of the sons of Clovis.

The image has haunted me
for years –
those rafted young men
ham strung, tendons burnt
at the order of a monstrous mother;
the bound feet
forever useless
seem large and white.

The mother, repentant,
has them laid
along the floating platform,
flowers and candles
by the murdered feet.
They will drift
along the Seine
slowly
to inevitable death.

My tendons are intact;
one day soon
will help carry me
along the Seine
which is my street.

Still I mourn for the sons of Clovis.

Froth and Bubble

Excuse

At the Hobart launch of Frank McCourt's latest book *Teacher Man*, he mentioned that his non-academic class proved to be very fluent and imaginative when forging parental excuse notes. He suggested the class write an excuse letter from Eve to God. The idea, to me, was irresistible.

A note from Eve

Dear God
I truly beg Your pardon
for my misdemeanour in the garden,
Your adder I found so seductive
I didn't know he was destructive –
his voice was honey, just like this-s
(later it became a hiss).
I tell You, Lord, I was beguiled,
as innocent as any child.

And that asp with voice like honey,
no doubt thought it very funny
when he caused my eyes to see
that utterly delightful tree,
and lied and bade me eat the fruit,
which, I must say, was really beaut,
and that is why I shared with Adam –
He didn't say, 'No thank you, Madam.'

That serpent had another meaning,
which I gather is demeaning,
but then a Freudian connotation
is an inference post-creation.

Anyway, I know we fell,
the fig leaves didn't serve us well,
but God, You did create the snake,
do You think 'twas *Your* mistake?

And look what's happened! A whole race
increasing at a dreadful pace,
still eating from the tree, you see,
so all the blame can't rest with me,
please may I have a small reprieve?
Blame Adam, too.

                        Yours truly,
                              Eve.

A reply to Eve

Dear Eve,
When I decided on Creation
You weren't there for consultation,
nor did I think My lovely snake
would of you such a victim make.
That silly Adam, catatonic,
was meant to be a friend platonic
but when he of the apple ate
of course you had to procreate.

I admit the naughty human race
is nothing but a right disgrace,
however it seems there soon will be
a sex that's neither he nor she.
I think you'll grant I've made amends
when thus My great Creation ends.
I state my case quite truthfully
And now sign off
                        Yours ruefully,
                              God.

Slick

Sticky tale twist

A VICTORIAN man who got stuck in a washing machine while naked has put his own spin on the tale, saying his rescue felt similar to being born.

Emergency services were called to the Mooroopna home of 20-year-old "Lawrence" on Saturday after he got wedged in his top-loader.

They used Lawrence's favourite olive oil to manoeuvre him out of the tight spot.

"'It was a bit like a birthing," he told a radio station yesterday.

'It just won't work,' said Henrietta,
'Time goes by and nothing's better;
Off I go to work each day
Leaving you at home to PLAY –
That's what you do although you swore
That you'd be writing much, much more,
But that is not my main complaint
(I never saw you as a saint)
For now I find that you're a BORE –
It's hard to love for evermore.'

'Nothing you do gives me surprise,
You peck my cheek then close your eyes
And go to sleep – and what is more,
Regale me with your raucous snore.
I tell you, I have had enough,
Tomorrow I will pack my stuff
And go to mother – last resort –
For all my ranting comes to naught.'
Off she went and slammed the door,
'Oh,' moaned Toby, 'never more...'

'Never more look into her eyes.'
Light bulb moment! 'I'll surprise
The girl, indeed I will,
Show her that I love her still.'

Towards the evening Toby stripped,
Into the washing machine he slipped –
Well, wriggled rather, but no matter –
Bit of luck he was no fatter.
'I don't need water or washing soda,
Just Adam's suit and this top loader;
Then she'll know I'm not a twit
But an artist with a ready wit.
When she comes home I'll leap upright,
'BOO!' I'll say as I stand full height.'

Crouching there he heard her key –
Anticipation and high glee!
Changing work clothes for something posher
Henrietta threw garb into the washer
I'm sure all readers will surmise
Awaiting her was SURE surprise.
On Toby's head, with eyes both staring,
Reposed the clothes his love was wearing,
On hold the poor lad's planned delight,
For then he found he was wedged quite tight.

He could not utter. 'BOO!' but 'HELP!'
Accompanied by an anguished yelp.
Henrietta rang emergency,
Said it was a matter of greatest urgency,
But as Toby tried to wiggle
She found it hard to curb a giggle.
Soon the helpful crew arrived,
With muscled arms and hands all strived
To pull poor Toby from his restriction
(I'll say nothing of his diction).

Strive they did without avail
But as the prisoner voiced a wail
Depressed by all the useless toil
A bright spark asked, 'Have you some oil?'
Toby thought of his cold pressed virgin,
Used to baste such things as sturgeon.
Never mind, he must be freed,
So, suppressing all his greed
He told them it's exact location
So they could start the operation.
They found the oil, they poured it on him,
Eased his arms and freed each limb.

Soon he was able to proudly stand,
Though not exactly as he had planned,
But here he was in shining glory
(With fodder for another story)
And he could tell from Etta's eyes,
She quite approved this great surprise.
He rose to fame, was in the paper,
Making the most of his rash caper.
Reporters were with laughter torn
When he said, 'It felt like being born.'

Never the bride

I thought of you lately, Miriam Slater,
I don't like to think that I've been a base hater
But as our school classes moved upwards, I
                                          reckoned
You would come first and I would come second.

What REALLY did it, I think, were those numbers.
I'll bet you said tables in your night slumbers.
And all those sheep were, I'm sure, multiplied,
And then, just for fun, you'd add and divide.

While MY dreams were spattered with colons and
                                           dashes
And queries and dots and commas like rashes.
Useful devices for good compositions,
No good at all for math propositions.

Oh, Miriam Slater, where are you now?
Are you top notch and taking your bow?
Did you climb high on the corporate ladder
Or become rich, a society gadder?

Or are you in heaven with halo all shiny?
First class, of course, while MINE will be tiny.
But, don't you see, we'll have reached the
                                           same place,
It will then be made plain how pointless the race.
Heaven, of course, is with geniuses fecund,
But God always has time for those who come
                                           second.

To LG – a kind of ode

You gave me comfort, kept me pure;
Words cannot conjure your allure.
Your devotion never foundered –
You, so white and nicely rounded.

I valued your simplicity
Yet joined in the complicity
To wrench you from your long-held moorings,
And curb your sometimes wild outpourings.

When brutish men came through the door
No watery torrents did you pour.
'Oh, life's good,' you dared remind me –
Such a sound philosophy.

Like a modern Mata Hari,
Slick and shiny, multi-starry,
Your replacement's no has-been –
Farewell, my one-star washing machine.

LG: the brand of washing machine – 'Life's Good'

A rhyme in praise of the semicolon

There is a trend contemporaneous
To ban the mark some think extraneous,
And I have struggled to pen a sonnet,
To bring to air my thoughts upon it;
But I'm no Wordsworth and my grief
Needs be pedestrian for relief.

Today's grammarians have stolen
The useful, wonderful semi-colon.
I think that this has come to be
In the modern struggle for brevity.
A sentence must be sharp and short,
No need for marks of any sort.

What if by chance one reads some prose
(In a text quite olden, I suppose)
Surely one would grateful be
A punctuation mark to see?
Should we need to gulp for air
More than a comma needs be there.

You'll recall, if you are not a dunce,
There was a semicolon once;
In any case it deserves renown
Since it's a comma with a crown,
But let me close before you flee
Filled to the top with gross ennui –

I'm glad this hasn't had the chop –
The absolutely vital, sweet FULL STOP.

Hot lips – a cautionary tale

No doubt you have heard of a Spicy Romance?
I thought I should like one but hadn't the chance.
I wasn't quite sure of what it comprised
And felt, should I learn, it would leave me surprised.

However, my lover, one night in a hurry.
Decided our menu should feature a curry,
So in went the powders of curry and chilli,
In quantities most would consider quite silly.

The mountain of rice it accompanied looked splendid
And I eagerly ate just as much as my man did.
Much later our lips (still quite hot) coincided,
My love looked bemused and anon, he decided
My kiss tasted good – was it chutney or curry?
He couldn't exactly decide in a hurry.

He kissed me once more and again licked his lips
With the joy of the bee as the nectar it sips.
I thought it was I that the bliss had evoked,
But no! cert 'twas the flavour provoked
upward glance of the eye, the smile most benign –
This the Spicy Romance I wished to be mine?

So to girls who aspire to the spicy and torrid
This truthful account may sound rather horrid.
I am sure that you feel, dear Madam or Miss,
That unflavoured kisses should give your man bliss.

So here's the advice that I give out of hand:
Your best courting diet must always be bland.
True the infant-mild food will be nothing to savour,
But your kiss will be claimed for its very own flavour!

'When I'm old I shall wear purple'

Jenny Joseph

We say we'll wear purple when we're old
but we don't.
Religion forbids it.
Our elders, Protestant or Catholic,
issued a fiat,
a ban on lunatic purple
and harlot red or black,
(especially in satin).
We must not draw attention to ourselves;
wear our skirts too short
or our necklines too low.

Now, shiny is 'in',
and so are breasts
and other parts less tastefully displayed;
and sequins, beads and all that glitters.
I'm not brave
but the wild within me steps out,
a fearless wraith
in a red velvet jacket
and with a susurrus of purple taffeta
spangled with crystals.

Sour grapes

I often pray for the revival
Of bodies built for long survival;
I guarantee those breasts of Helen's
Were quite as large as ripest melons.

Bring back the tummy nicely mounded
And ample thighs all white and rounded.
When will the beauty buffs declare
The charms of an ample derrière?

Herrick's 'vibrations two way free'
Are what a female rear should be.
Come the famine the nicely plumpish
Will know its good to be right lumpish

And call upon the extra storage
Without the need for desperate forage.
Ironically, they'll then be svelte,
Their skinny sisters naught but pelt.

The Resolution of a Problem

I thought that most folk knew the useful Celtic spurtle,
Like tartan and the haggis and things Scots like to hurtle,
But now I know for sure that this is not the case,
And it's hard to find the thingummy in any darned place.

Lately, off I went to the well-stocked Habitat,
I asked for a spurtle. 'Madam, what is THAT?'
'You know, a thing for stirring breakfast porridge.'
The assistant shook her head and then went off to forage.

Returning, she asked me for a clear, succinct description;
It wasn't really easy to comply with this prescription.
'Like a copper stick, but short,' was my crystalline reply;
Still obvious bewilderment and a very heavy sigh.

'And pray what is a copper stick?' the poor assistant queried,
But I'm afraid that by this time, I felt extremely wearied.
It's likeness to a broom handle I have too late digested,
Though grateful to some friends for the simile suggested.

Now I have investigated yet another place;
I'm delighted to report that it's quite a different case.
At last my search has ended in the purchase of a spurtle,
And for added delectation it's entirely made of myrtle.

Downfall

You raise your jewelled feathers,
shake them and advance,
and I, poor silly peahen,
though familiar with your dance,
capitulate.

www.ingramcontent.com/pod-product-compliance
Lightning Source LLC
Chambersburg PA
CBHW062202100526
44589CB00014B/1916